REUNION

REUNION
Deanna Young

Brick Books

Library and Archives Canada Cataloguing in Publication

Young, Deanna, 1964–, author
Reunion / Deanna Young.

Poems.
Issued in print and electronic formats.
ISBN 978-1-77131-488-6 (softcover).—ISBN 978-1-77131-490-9 (PDF).—
ISBN 978-1-77131-489-3 (EPUB)

I. Title.

PS8597.O592R48 2018   C811'.54   C2018-902173-X
C2018-902174-8

Second printing: June, 2019

We acknowledge the Canada Council for the Arts, the Government of
Canada through the Canada Book Fund, and the Ontario Arts Council for
their support of our publishing program.

The author photo was taken by Alice Young.
The book is set in Scala.
Design and layout by Marijke Friesen.

Printed and bound by Coach House Printing.

Brick Books
431 Boler Road, Box 20081
London, Ontario N6K 4G6

www.brickbooks.ca

Dedication

And this, a story
For all the children whose lives
Begin burning down
Though the lamp's just been lit—

Who ask themselves
Daily, *Why be born for this?*
Who crawl under the smoke
But don't find the door.

For those who survive, hope.
For the others, infinite love.

My tongue, every atom of my blood, form'd from this soil, this air,
Born here of parents born here from parents the same, and their
parents the same . . .

—Walt Whitman

We were blessed by the forlorn
Forsaken and abused

—Lucinda Williams

Contents

Ghost Prayer

Let the ghosts greet you.
Go to the crossroads
and wait till you hear
the ruffled breath of their horses.

They are coming
because they know you're there.
Welcome them as you would
your young self, long lost—

like breezes let them in.
Stand in the open doorways
to catch their empty sleeves
as they pass from room to room.

They've seen enough to know
it won't be easy. Love
and mercy, mercy and love—
Let them speak first

and with your living body listen.

Like Bees

Look out across the plunging, silver sea
of canola stubble. Fields unfurling into the past—
so many years of production behind them.

Winter gone, another coming,
but for now the earth grows warm.

The dun and yellow groves
below are greening.

Like bees
the voices swarm.

●

Here is a small amount of my life
I want to give you.

It's not water, it's not sand. Still,
it's falling through my fingers.

Rain Psalm

And the clouds gave way, and the generations
of pained voices fell, exhausted, into the merciful lap

of the earth, into the furrows of the worried fields.
And the warmth of the black soil turned them

to mist, the mist to the last breath of a story
rising out of the past. And the seeds, dusty

suitcases we knew to be secreted in the land
by faeries, creaked open, raising yellow hands

into the buzz and industry of an early June morning
in Middlesex County, testing the air. And the fat robins

in orange shirts and neat grey jackets were there
to greet the young shoots, and hopped beside them,

tugging glistening worms from the ears of the ground
ripe with manure, till the sun grew hot, and the roar

of the tractor rose from the drive shed. And there
in coveralls, the man named Jake, *Jacobus*, stepfather

of cousin Johnny, who cared for the land like it was
his own—his own child or dog or soul. And lo,

the new day of labour and growth was begun.

Holy Ghost

We had no paper
then, or we had

no pen, or no words. How
to say it. We had

no voice. No listeners.
Just deaf night

and the flames that chased us
up the stairs, that

found us
panting, singed. There was

no story then, no
greater myth. It was just

our life. No big
picture. No art

but the Bible. No thought
but that the Lord must have made

some mistake, our souls
in error. We went

into the closet willingly—it was
a game—

as into a time machine.
More in hope

than faith. In there
saw only starless space.

We prayed.
When I open this door

let it be
some other place.

There was music
though, astounding.

It flowed from the stereo
and filled the house

like Jesus. It was
Aretha in raiment of gold

and Elvis the King.
It flew into us like grace and shook

our spirits loose. We fell
to the floor like change, all

scattered silver. There
gathered ourselves

into swords of light, there rose
and followed the tambourines

into the shimmering
forest-mind

where we could think.
We walked among

the years like trees
and, trembling, came

to a sky-filled river.
Stepped into its rush like deer

to drink, cold wonder
pulling at our legs.

We gave ourselves up
for lost, raised our arms like thieves—

Sun lit the blood
of our fingertips, field sparrows

sang our names—and thus
in rapture

were we saved.

Ballad of the Central Hotel

John, where are you going?
I'm going to hell.
Why don't you join me?
It's warmer down there.

John, what will you do there?
I'll drink till I'm hammered
Then drink till I'm plastered
And fall down the stairs.

The waitresses know me,
The boys'll be waiting.
Jim Currie, Bill Hodgins,
Bob Norton, John Cain—Hell!

The whole volunteer fire brigade, brigade,
The whole friggin' fire brigade!

But you're banned from the station,
Kicked out of the Masons,
You're out of a job
And haven't been paid.

Shut yer face, useless woman.
Like I said, you're insane.
Think I'll call up the pigs
To come cart you away.

The kids'll be farmed out
And treated like slaves,
And your dear dead dad
Will turn black in his grave—Oh!

Your dad'll go soft in his grave, his grave,
The sucker will rot in his grave.

John, what will I do here
Without any car?
Damned if I know, bitch,
And damned if I care.

I'll be down at the Central,
And don't come and get me.
You can rag all you want,
I'll be home when I'm ready.

I'll be drinking the mortgage
And drinking the groceries.
By supper, by Christ,
I'll be down on all fours—like a hound,

I'll be well on my way, my way,
By then I'll be feelin' the flames—

Reunion

My small body then
at the top of the stairs

in its flannel nightie.

Bones gone to water inside my legs.

While below in the guts of the house
the lions roared.

A door was slammed

and all the downy sparrows,
the messengers of luck, laughter, spring,

confidence and ease,

flew out the windows of my ears,
my eyes and mouth.

The house
now empty.

Only the family
of shiny black bugs

living on what in the basement?

The dogs asleep in the hallway
woke

and knew they'd been abandoned.

Witness

Set me down, dear angel, in that kitchen again
for one blinding moment

it's all I could take
of that torch in my face

that I might again bear witness
to the monstrous

speech of my father
which cannot be written down

lest it knock at our skulls
with a field stone

lest it wrap its hands
around our bendy necks

and the children find us
there

before school in the morning
purple sky at the window

blood on the table and blood on the floor

Ken

Christmas day he reads *The Donnellys Must Die* by Orlo Miller until his eyes are wooden. 1962. A gift from his eldest daughter. The front page signed in rough blue script by the author himself. He turns the book over in his hands. A warm, flat stone.

It had happened in his father's time, not ten miles east of here at Lucan, where his daughter's new friend has people. An old farmer and four of his family, murdered in their bedclothes. The place set fire.

He leans in closer to the lamp. Four o'clock, the herd fed, sun bleeding out behind the drive shed. Snow dust swirling across the fields, lost in itself. That purple light in Heaven.

Images bob in his mind, like lanterns among trees at evening. A rap at the door, and the killer strides in. A mumbling host of vigilantes on black horses in the lane.

They had no warrant. And no moon to witness.

But look: here the table is set so proudly. The white cloth, and a mound of golden dinner rolls. A bowl of buttered peas and the bird's breast high and crispy. A crystal dish aglitter with pearl onions, dill pickles, beets. On his plate a drift of potatoes doused in gravy. Despair licks up the walls inside his head.

The world is a net of joys and sorrows and we are caught in it, with no more chance than a perch on sand. The births of our children and then the worry. Long years bent to their well-being burnt down in a night by the jokers they marry.

There remain, after all his prayers, the voices. The same, he's sure, that tormented his uncle, who cradled his own head in wind-picked hands ten winters before taking down the rifle. Which are worse, he wonders, as the holiday cheer bubbles around him, the troubles that come knocking, or the ones already inside.

He'll finish the book this night then lie in its thrall.

To be lured from your bed at that ungodly hour, the life knocked from you. Your gurgling body watching from the floor as they go after your wife and kin. The cries of your niece upstairs. The orange ghosts dancing in your windows.

Sleep

There are the early hours
when the front room is washed
in a pink light.

It is the newborn day
still sleeping

on a blanket of blue water.

I walk through this light
on my way to the bathroom

and it falls on me, all around me.

I look down and see that my hands
are pink,

my bare feet.

My grandparents knew this light.

They rose routinely
like this—the birds already up
and busy—and went down to find it waiting
in their front room.

Out their window, the rosy band
spread richly over the black field
becoming green.

Their June sea.

When they looked at each other
the light was on their faces—the whole room

like this room, washed
in tenderness and glory.

Until worry
arrived,

arrives.

Conversations I had on the phone last night
still with me. Running into the nooks
of my woken brain
like water.

And thus stalled at the glowing hinge
of day, I falter.

It is the crippled daughter
we must tend to,

though our love makes us tired.

All we want
is to go back to bed.

For a few moments
we stand in her light

and struggle with our thoughts.

Sleep wants us
to let her die.

Our own beloved daughter.

Sleep wants us
all to itself.

We Gather

In daylight we walk upon the land
like living children, a sunburnt tribe towards the woods
where light flashes among the trees like money.

Drawn to where the cow lies, her clean skull resting
on its pillow of musty leaves. White rib cage
a church where faeries pray

for their delicate lives, minutely sing.
In exile, we gather solemnly there to worship
what might lie beyond this place, where the cow

in her devastation now peacefully lives.
Where later, in pools of moonlight, we will swim,
fear lapping at our beds. For shore

we will swim, the other side, that shimmering
pasture where the cow still lows, still grazes. Wet grass
flecked white and yellow, the sweetest buds.

Sheila Margaret

In love with the heft and swing of letters,
that unbound *S*, broad-shouldered *H*,
she'd scatter grain for the hens in the shape of her name
so that when they fell in, she'd be revealed to herself
in feathers, future fame spelled out plain

as dirt. Rhode Island Reds in ruffled skirts.
Give us an *E*! Give us an *I*! *L*! *A*!
Though drawn to the yard, the barn, her father,
she knew how swiftly
the axe could fall. *Sheila!* Her mother

on the porch in flowered housedress,
eternal apron.

Catch up one of those birds for supper!

But Lord, which one.

Dark

comes up behind.
Guess who? The old
hands over the eyes.
He presses a little
into Dawn's back, in front
of all. He gives her
a special name
she must then answer to.
Clever Dark accomplishes
much of his handiwork
by day—dim Light
in the kitchen crying
into her Nescafé or frying
him up some eggs—
then finishes the job
at night. His face blue
from the aquarium
that spans a wall,
Dark watches the quilt
move up and down.
Dawn snoozing
on the chesterfield.
He uses the name
to wake her. *Up you get.*
Then steps hard
on her toe for quiet.

Supper Prayer

And here is the wallpaper
that holds our gaze at supper, and our thoughts
in their place, lest these too be corrupted
by what has happened to us
during the day.

The same sparrow resting there and there
among the sprouting branches.

And here a welcome plate
of food, dear Lord, our sustenance and distraction,
again to keep away the grumblings
of despair that might otherwise
fill our mouths.

That none would pierce the gentle evening
with a forked tongue.

And here, Lord, spoken
around the table, the names, be they blessed or damned,
of parents and their parents, cousins near
and distant, of those they've married,
and of our neighbours.

And of the blameless children sprouting
like beans in the garden.

For it is in the names
and in the naming, Lord, in the myths and buried
deeds that we shall find the saved seeds

of our selves, and of our sorrow,
and not solely in thee.

>   *Though the truth arrive on its horse in time*
>   *and without invitation.*

Lilac

Barefoot over warm grass
towards the lilac, your calling voice

fresh air open window
a clean bathroom

you calling my name
but not exactly, some mash
of mine and his

I want to be with you Aunt
in the green waves, congregations
of flowery hats

out there in the sparkling
afternoon, your lilac calling
my almost-name

call again and I'll find you—no!
you come find me

I'm upstairs
in this blanket box, cedar brain of me
safe and clean

on the bed my body
being touched

my brown board body my sun-
stroked mind

and the bees in me humming darkly
against the screen

they ping and ping

fall down climb up
and ping

come find me Aunt

—no don't! if you do
you will die—he told me

blanket-box brain
bed-body—hush-hush

from the ceiling, hush-hush
now honey, it'll soon
be done

now you've stopped
calling—you might
be coming

screen door creaking—
it's bad to be here

I must get downstairs
without you knowing

to the dough we set to rise
in the big blue bowl

but no legs no tongue no

voice no name

there I go! lawn-soul lawn-soul lawn-soul

there I go lawn-soul-lawn-soul—

Sermon on the House

... As the Native peoples understand that the land and everything in it has a spirit which must be respected, so we must understand that the house and everything in it, the plumb doors and wavy windows, the water-stained ceilings and creaking floors, airless closets and narrow halls all have a spirit that we must cherish. For as we inhabit our houses, so they, trusting, place their store in us.

And let this understanding be the practiced faith and solace of the beleaguered mother called to raise her children in a house rocked like a boat on a wind-torn lake. In the long night of her misfortune, let her keep the faith that children require shelter from storms and shielding from predators, that they require secure and peaceful spaces in which to grow, unafraid and unmolested, into whom they were meant to become, and without cruel interference.

For it is only in the rested waking, in the peace of the table and the daily bread-breaking, in the routine of leaving and returning home unafraid at the end of each day—yea, in the steady confidence of days—and again in the chaste embrace of needed sleep, that children may endure and thrive.

Therefore, praise be to the foundation, to the solid bricks and mending mortar, to the square joists and supporting beams; praise to the furnace and to the newspaper that is the insulation; praise to the rooftop that stands between the family and the indifferent weather, to the mailbox that waits, to the number by the door, and to the heroic name of the street—may we carry it with us like a coin in our pocket when we go, and may that coin give some small comfort to our grasping hands.

But first, let us rejoice in the very concept of the house, whether it is there for us now, once was, or may one day be. When adrift on the wide lake of insecurity, then rejoice in those who call from the shore, who open their doors and invite us in, as we may, any of us, one day be wanderers in need of roof and cup. Rejoice, above all, in the firm embrace of walls; in their compassion and generosity are they wondrous—as the sky that gives freely its light and rain is wondrous. Rejoice, then, in the benefaction of community, for it is community that shall be our children's saving grace.

Yea, for the house and all it holds, be thankful. Honour its spirit, for it is sacred. Care for the house that is your self and soul, and for the houses of your neighbours, for those beside you and those on the other side of the road. Care for the houses far beyond your fences—the shacks and tenements, the crowded tents—for all those close and distant.

In this way, care for yourself and for one another. Care for the children and for the mother, and for the father who was once a child, forever and ever, amen.

Rain Song

And the voices came pouring
Like rain, like rain, and the rain,
It soothed the ground.

And the apples grew red
In the orchard again, and the wind
Sang all around!

Tiny

When I was born they wrapped me
in a towel and set me in a roaster
in the oven. It was just warm
and they left the door open.
It was that cold in the house
and I was that small.

Gertrude, my mother called me,
but Tiny stuck. It suited me well
till the weight came on
around thirteen.

And wouldn't I end up
big as a house.

Best day of my life
was marrying Glenn.
Get me out of this place, I told him—

with my brothers all fighting
for food like rats and my sisters
hissing like snakes.

Glenn built us a home
with his own two hands
and the babies started coming.

I always liked *D*s, so I named them:
Debbie, David, Denise, Darren, Darryl.
The last one I lost
I would've called Dean.

Sure, the house was full of cracks
and the floors weren't level.

Glenn got what he could
from the dump for free
and the rest he found on the street.

From the road at night
when the lights were on
you could tell where the wall joints
didn't quite meet.

That time in the storm
when the village went dark
and you came with your dad
and sisters to sleep

'cause we had the stove for heat

—your poor mother stuck
at the deboning plant in St. Marys—

and I gave you a drink
of our stinky well water and told you,
Don't worry, it's safe,

I thought,
Such a scared little thing.

I knew your dad was as bad
as they come, but what could I do.
He was my brother.

The Shillelagh

Where is my father?
He's at the Shillelagh.
How long has he been there?
Nearly all your drear life.

Your mother can't fetch him,
He's pissed up and surly—
You in with the coppers
Or writing a book?

But who is there with him?
Your cousin, young Cheri,
Who got kicked in the gut,
Now she can't have a baby.

You know how she likes
To carouse with the fellas.
Still, you don't hurt a lady—
It's just not right.

But—

No more buts, that's a good girl.
Enough with the questions.
The bed bugs are starved—
Kiss your uncle goodnight.

Whips and Scorns

So here is Bob Norton, my father's friend, and here
the belt that whips the children. I back up
when he slips it out of his waistband and takes a shot
at his own hand, to see if it's working.

He bought the Donnelly place in '74
but not, as he'll tell you, the bull. When *that clown*
Stompin' Tom came around with a crew, Bob grabbed the .22
and told them, *This ain't no circus, get off my land.*

We all shoulda heard him. Young Robbie's
at the barn right now, tormenting kittens. Bob and the missus
don't know where he gets it—the mean streak.
When the charge from the fence

jumps right through the cat and snaps
its teeth at Robbie instead, Bob howls, *That'll serve ya!*
We all like Bob then, kinda. Despite the belt
and everything else, I sometimes think I prefer him

to my own father. Then again, better go
with the devil you know. Anyway Tracy is nice. Her stomach
is flatter than mine, her hair longer, and one day she'll marry
a rich businessman. Nights I stay over she likes

to compare vaginas—*Wanna see mine? Okay . . . not really—*
but is quickly distracted by ghosts. Dead Donnellys
moan inside the wall our bed touches. They are trapped
in this mortal coil and so are we.

Picking Stones

I followed along with the others
under the sun's strict gaze:

Who among you will last till lunch?

I wanted to prove myself worthy.

Uncle Jake up ahead on the tractor
looking back over his shoulder
to keep the lines straight.
The faith.

Rex the German shepherd
was tied up always. In a coat
of flies, in sun and shade, he was there
to keep away the foxes.

The chain looked strong.

Grain in the silo with its honey breath.

One false step—
As explained to me by Johnny.

He knew of a man who'd been buried alive.

Cousin, four years older, his shoes had soles
three inches high, his room

a black-and-white homage to Kiss.

I stood in the doorway in awe
of something.

Self-expression.

At the time,
I didn't know why I stood there.

Back then I could never find words
for what I saw.

Titty Ditty

The Bare Ones are a band
Without the benefit of tops.
They strum and sing
And swing their things,
The bouncing never stops!

They're down at the Shillelagh
Every Friday night till one.
My sage advice
Is dump your wife
And come and join the fun!

Gentle Evening

Evening cannot wait.
She is pressing her hands to her chest
as if to say, *Hear me.* No one is listening.

I am turning purple, she pleads,
I will be indigo soon—indigo! She fears
a life of dying

routinely like this,
unseen and unremarked upon,
only to wake again daily, clothed wetly

in black, in the pit
of the well out back. For to call and be heard
is to live—only these.

No, Evening must wait
each day for the sun to turn
and lock the cupboard, and drop the key

in her apron pocket,
before she can even begin to hope—
only for the hour to darken

utterly again and quickly, as surest night
steps from behind the drive shed
to suck the rose from her cheek.

Oh gentle Evening, unwelcome
as the truth at table. Unspoken to for days,
for draining weeks, as she grows

up, and old—God-given light
so cruelly wasted.

Her dimming life,
this room.

The Lamp

What, when resurrection doesn't happen,
When the blown flame sputters, and dies?
Who will carry the lamp then, cold and useless?
Why did it ever burn? Why was it lit?

There are the living and the departed,
The held ones and the discarded.
And there, the shadows that drift among us.
How will we embrace them now?

Luckless, faultless, on Earth forsaken.
Lifted from their cradles, shaken.
The lamps that could not burn again—
What of them? What light in that darkness?

Jean Young, Matriarch, Speaks from the Grave

A skinny broad
with a thing for rubies.

Redhead. Or was I?
Five boys and five girls,

five swirled
down the drain in between.

I would argue
the hooks off drapes,

the butter from a cake,
and lick my fingers after.

Rye and water
my only comfort

after the doctor told me
to swear off sweets.

Diabetic, he claimed,
but oh, how I missed

my rye and ginger!
Bony and brash,

phony and rash—
they could call me

what they liked. And did.
Fried baloney and mash

for eleven on Sunday—what better
would you have done?

My man Fred more gone
on the railroad than not.

Each visit
another nine-month sentence.

When I passed by the gate
in '78, I expected

a decent turnout
and that's what I got. At Haskett's

the casket was closed
but not the case.

Don't think I wasn't listening.
It was dry tears

all around, a few bent noses
blown. And the windows

thrown wide like Mother's arms—
dozens of rough-winged swallows

darning the clear blue sky.
The birds that day, good God—

You'd have thought Cinderella
was lying there in state.

Make no mistake.
The night the dark angel, my prince,

came down, I cried,
Take me quick! And bloody hell,

the bugger did.

Baptist Luncheon

At fifteen
silence drawn like drapes
around the table

when the father
of the girl I'd befriended at school

to whom I clung in loneliness
in crowded halls and whose name
I now forget

turned to me:

Tell us, dear,
how your Christian walk is going.

Girl at Home

There is always the fear
of emerging from the bathroom, towel-wrapped,
to encounter a man

who's been listening for the clunk
of taps choked off, the shush
of water stopped.

When she peers into the hallway
—even decades later—and he is not,
thank God, there, still

she braces
for the dash to the bedroom,

droplets fleeing from her ankles.

What's that?
You've heard this before,
dear reader? This old complaint?

Perhaps
you should leave us then.

As I was saying.

Let us bow our heads
in silence now

for the morning she stepped
from behind the plastic curtain

to find drawn in the steam
of the vanity mirror

a message:

I see you're a woman now.

Anytime I want, is what he meant.

The Flame

I woke
And searched the lanes
Behind the houses.

I searched
And was afraid
What I might find.

I stalled
And so my courage
Went before me,

The courage
That had wavered
Long inside me

Flared up—a sturdy flame
That led me
Through the night.

How the Sounds Carry

Out here on a cloudy night
the dark is complete.

Not a skim of light
to coat what's in the room.

No hand floats
above my face. No hope of sleep.

Someone or something

must be over at the property
on the Coursey Line.

The dogs are angry
or excited, throwing themselves

at the chain-link
limits of their senses again.

Nancy

A shame,
We hardly knew her.
She had a pretty face.

My uncle wed
Then slew her—white-throated
Sparrows pled her case.

Her soul left
Through a keyhole. Her body
Left a stain.

Now here is Time, come
To take away her name.

And Eyes So Black

I love thee Wilma, with hair like silk,
Lips like cherries, skin like milk,
Your shell-like ears, your dainty hands,
And eyes so black, like frying pans.

—Fred Flintstone

93   Q. Now let's go on to this breaking of the ribs, would you describe that incident to me, what led up to this?

A. Well he'd come from out drinking and I was—

94   Q. When was this first of all?

A. Probably about five years ago. 1972.

95   Q. Go on.

A. He'd been out drinking and when he came home I just asked him where he'd been. I thought it was my place to ask him where he'd been and he said it was none of my goddamn business and so I don't know what happened. Prior to that we probably had a bit of an argument and he knocked me down and broke my ribs.

96   Q. You had a bit of an argument—probably had a bit of an argument or you did?

A. Verbal argument, yes.

97   Q. Did you ever hit your husband on the head with a frying pan?

A. No.

98   Q. Did you ever hit your husband with a frying pan?

A. No. I've hit him with a broom—I've hit him with a broom.

Kennedy Cousins

Debbie a maid
to her blind grandparents
who live down the lane.

David a poplar
at the edge of a field. If he's
thinking, he's not saying.

Denise a tease
with a nose-pinch
when speaking. *Neesie.*

Darren and Darryl
cutting worms in half
with a dime, though not meanly,

amazed how they squirm
and appear to live on, two worms
where once there was one.

Beds in the attic, sheets
hung up for walls. Ghosts shifting,
though mostly

friendly ones. Heads lolling
on pillows without any cases, grey
ticking, a waft of pee.

Just us worms
tucking in for the night, moonlight
scything the gloom above us.

Recrimination

I stand here this April morning, dear citizens
of Biddulph, and swear this truth: the cries

that ran through that house were unholy, the clamour
you heard and harm you suspected, the marks

on the arms of my mother, your call to action.
And yet you stood by. You closed your drapes

and extinguished your lamps. In the morning,
mist hung in the air, as it does here today, a lamentation

risen from the lawn. And was your blood so chilled
that thoughts of the children dwelling in that

yellow house on George Street could not
unstop the fair accusations in your throats?

Could not one of you have gone to him, and said,
John, this is wrong. Were you not duty-bound

to knock at the door of that madness?
I am looking at all of you here today, a blanket of light

draped over us at this crossroads, the sun still rising.
Go home with these thoughts in your minds.

And blessings be eternal on any of you who did
step forward then—the righteous. Though I did not

know you, I am here by your kindness. In the name
of the mother, the daughters, and the small black dog.

What Voice

What holds me stiff
In fright, what shakes me.

What takes me by the shoulders
And warns, *Don't tell,*

In a whisper. What makes me.
What steers me

To the cellar door
Where none will find me,

What calls
From across the field

With lies
Of my young son and daughters.

With its hooked
Finger, what draws me

Like a sheep
Towards a slick hole.

What breaks
My leg, my spirit,

And leaves me to suffer.
What voice

Stands over me
in the trap of night.

4:00 a.m.

There is an hour
God lets us sleep through.

She attends us there,
frightened mother.

When we wake at four,
a shard of it

in our eye,
she lays a hand

on our forehead,
leans down

to breathe in the sweat
behind our ear.

The Holy Bottle

Young John Young was a mean old dad,
He sucked raw eggs and his feet smelled bad.
He kissed the bottle and he cussed his wife
And never said boo when he wrecked our life.

Lola

In the courtyard after lunch, residents take the sun, steel rims of their wheelchairs gleaming. Despite the spectre of Death lurking at the end of every polished hallway, the nursing home is a spiritless place. Before here it was the bungalow in Ailsa Craig. Before that, the farm, where for twenty-four years she slept beside a man she loved, worked *like the devil* from dawn till night, raised three children of her own and fostered several more. *Home*, she still calls it.

On a wet November morning I dial the old number. *Mercy, is that you honey?* I picture her recliner set back from the TV. Across the room, her roommate, a featherless bird of ninety pounds, is sunk in her own chair before her own murmuring screen. Geraniums climb the window, pressing red faces and green hands against the glass. We talk of relatives, the dead and living, most I never knew or don't recall meeting. When it comes time to say goodbye, there it is again, the watery *You know I think about you honey*—a rope thrown toward me as the receiver leaves my ear.

There's a picture of us in matching aprons when I was three. Me and this woman who never once wore slacks or drank wine, who covered her mouth to stifle a laugh when I told her *Jiminy Cricket!* was code for *Jesus Christ*.

Why do I never have the presence of mind to stop, and ask, *What is it, Grandma? Why so sad?* The question pressing itself to my mouth like a hand.

Riddle

I peer down the throat
With a blind eye.

I explode in that well,
Emerge dripping, but whole.

I make no sound
Though your ears ring.

Though you tell,
No one will save you.

Visit, 4:00 a.m.

Last night my father
showed up in my dream.

I knew him by his back and wide shoulders.
His head of curly black hair
none of us inherited.

We were doing this dance,
he and I, among rooms
that were all connected, in a circle.

Him unwilling to face me
and me, indignant.

My son was at the table
doing homework.

My father would stop his roaming
to peer over the boy's shoulder
and then move on.

I kept watch
from behind the glass of my dream.

He knew I was there.

My son bent over his work
unaware of the ghost. I did not believe
he was in any danger.

I watched only
for any sign of love
for the boy

who looks so much
like me at eight.

I don't think I'll see him again.

My father rarely spoke to me,
never met my eyes
if he could help it.

He never touched me
either—I just want to make that
perfectly clear—

not after the time
he lifted me from my crib
and threw me at the wall
like a cat.

As a brutalized man
does a cat.

My young mother
who had, until recently, never known violence,
rushing in, blood vessels bursting
around her eyes,
a kitchen knife.

The ensuing scene.

Ballad of Young John

He drives around the Legion twice.
He said he wouldn't do it.
But the night is hot, his brain like ice,
And in his heart he knew it.

He'd like to be the noble type
That puts his family first.
He knows a few who preach that hype,
But they don't know his thirst.

It's cool inside, the lights hung low,
Sunlight slicing through the blind . . .
If supper's on the table cold
It doesn't cross his pickled mind.

If he sticks to beer, he'll soon be home
To salute the bejesus wife.
If he starts in on the hard stuff, though,
It could get ugly, it could mean life.

Behind the bar, the mirror warns,
John, you've had enough.
Take it easy, pal, it's under control.
—And the wife, she likes it rough!

The spinny stars, the tacky breeze—
A bloody lip, red spit, and then—
The car won't start, he's lost the keys—
And couldn't say who or why or when . . .

He couldn't say how it all began
Or where it all might end.

Twilight

Now that the scars are silvered

the skin of her forearms thinned

now that the ruins are smoking, distant

her dear horse maimed

now that the voices have gorged

themselves on shame

and are nearly sated

her child-self

steps from the bedroom

still expecting blame

Amends

Now open the back door—hurry.
Go out to the well, the grass
damp, sun low, the side yard
pooled with shadow. The tin cup
is there, its tang of metal.
Is it still blood in your mouth
or ancient water? Your old name
like fireflies everywhere. Now
lower the rope. Make amends
for the ones who could not.

Lamb

The voices were small, insistent
and infinitely patient

in the years following
Rilke's abrupt instruction:

You must change your life.

I did not want to disrupt my life.

I called in sick.

I washed the dishes scattered across the countertop
like bewildered migrants.

I wiped the countertop
and stood back.

I went into the basement

and took a piece of lamb—the flesh of an animal
that had been born for slaughter, a portion
of its body

wrapped in brown paper and held
for months in a freezer—

I took it with a vow
to make soup.

His words
at my heels as usual.

... for here there is no place
that does not see you.

Cradling the package, I ascended the wooden steps
and left it to thaw
on the clean countertop.

In the living room
I picked up a book—not Rilke
this time, but one of the others wandering
in that camp of hallowed spirits—

and flopped down on the couch.

The first poem said
change your life, in its way.

The second
said change your life. And so on.

To leave the lover
and still have him.

To leave the children
and still be their mother, daily.

The answer
did not come.

It would not come
forth willingly, I saw.

Like a wild horse
or beaten dog, it would not step forward

until I showed it my empty hands.

First
I would have to drop
what was in my hands.

Then only
if I stood absolutely still

and offered my palm slowly
to its wet nose

might it incline its head.

I thought of the lamb,
in its death still something. Its power
over me. How sacred
my duty.

As I lay there on the couch
I bargained feebly,

weighing each thing I thought I loved
against the ache.

Early

Before five the birds begin.
They cannot wait, have no reason to wait,
and today I share their impatience and wake with them.
They are hidden among the still-dark trees
as I am hidden in this still-dark room.

Today they will do whatever it is
they desire. They have their routine, which cannot
be put off, and not once have they wished it could be.
Whereas soon I will ride a bus downtown
to brood in a carpeted office.

I must take them with me. In my head
I will build a nest where birds can thrive, an oaken crook
high above a dew-wet yard, and a bath
of rainwater brimming. How
to entice them. Come in,

dear warbling ones, I promise you
all that you wake for each day: the pink worms
of my worry, white maggots of my dread. If you will give me
one blithe song, one swooping day. I beg you,
come with me or let me stay.

Reunion

Sister Pat greets me
and shows me where to put my boots.

With whispers
she leads me to my room.

One window faces the river, high
and startling.

The other,
a crowd of blue spruce.

I lock the door behind her.

I can't help it.

●

An hour of accusing sunlight
in which I lay out books and papers,
stare.

A walk, maybe.

But the March sky turns,
drunken,

and throws down fistfuls of hail.

The clear stones scramble over the porch roof
below my window

like crowds running for cover
where there is no cover.

I lie down to nap

and the guilt lies on top of me.

•

A dirt road with no houses for a long way.

A truck, growling,
approaches from behind.

Passes.

Two young men,
eyes shadowed by baseball caps.

I hide the pill
under my tongue

like a mental patient.

•

At last a house,
but leaning drastically.

Black cedar shingles,
rotted. It can't be real.

An iron hand pump in the yard.

I make tracks
through the gravelly snow

alongside cloven tracks.

A single deer.

Fawn coat. Earlier,
her breath on the window.

Blankets folded
on the backs of armchairs.

A table with a red cloth and a vase
of plastic flowers. Lifeless,
deathless.

Trespassers
will be clubbed and dragged into the trees.

●

Sunlight exalts the chapel room.

On the Bible stand, the Song of Songs.

Alone, I mouth a verse
then two. My heart responds.

Back in my room
I read the whole book, the Goods News version

not nearly as good as the roiling
King James.

Thou art beautiful, O my love, as Tirzah, comely as Jerusalem,
terrible as an army with banners.

As I finish, the sky shudders,
sends down silver necklaces.

•

After two days I understand
that this is hard.

I would like to speak
out loud to someone now,

to sit across from them
and watch them

try to talk me down.

•

In my right side, a tiny pain
I've been observing for months.

A vague, intermittent twinge.

Doctors don't have time for such delusions.

There are too many others so close to death
they can smell its breath.

Best wait.

•

A revelation:

I essentially don't like myself
and there's no amount of poetry
can fix that.

No amount of walking.

Of wine.

•

On the far river bank, Jealousy and Rage
chase thought-rabbits

mercilessly
toward their basement apartments.

While beneath my other window,
the huddling spruce.

There
Insecurity and Envy nest,

grooming each other's feathers.

•

Even here, in retreat, I set myself tasks
then carry them out.

Later, when I look at the list

—*Inferno*, lunch, abandoned
church/cemetery, walk hill past bridge—

I see that it is meaningless.

My life
a make-work project.

·

By day three
I have run out of similes.

Seven hundred years ago
Dante used up most of them

and then one hundred years ago
Rilke took the last one.

No more metaphors either.

The shelf is not bare
because there is no shelf.

·

After lunch, I crest the hill and see
that I am more than halfway through my life.
It's undeniable.

I trace the river west
to its apparent end.

Sun presses its cigarette
into my eyes.

But here, by my side,
my faithful dogs: Love
and Fear.

Who would I be without them?

●

Heading back wind-whipped,
hunched and hooded,

and there, ahead of me on the bridge,
a husky shadow.

Where have you been?

The river underneath is fast, throwing gold darts of sunlight
back up at the sky.

Busy.

Everything burnished.

●

On the fourth day,
the moon's faint, sideways grin.

I tighten the cap
on the leftover wine,

bid my small room goodbye
as though it were human,

and wait in the vestibule for my ride.

The ban lifted, Sister Pat tells me
how she worked for many years in Peru.

Low, coastal regions, she clarifies,
not the mountains.

It's where we wanted to be.
Among the very poor.

So,
she has done it.

What she wanted to do.

●

In the car on the way home
I practice on my husband.

Saying only nice things
in a nice way.

How I imagine
I might have been.

My performance
stiff, a little heartbreaking.

●

That night I hover
over sleep,

near dawn succumb

to the dust of bare plywood
under bare feet. The upstairs hall

of the yellow house on George Street.

The house
inside me.

In the kitchen, burlap walls
painted harvest gold. A room of straw.

The catch

and hiss of a match.

●

The survivors
are in the basement.

Happy soul, thy days are ended,
All thy mourning days below . . .

My brethren.

My shining
black bugs. So resilient.

Grown large
as men, in fine, dark suits,
they form a circle. I am not afraid
and join them.

Go, by angel guards attended,
To the sight of Jesus go!

Solemn as space,

our hymn, our hum, a song
to mourn

the warm-blooded creatures
thrashing about

and whimpering above.

The Gully

It lives behind the house, it hums
and sighs. A snaking creek where willful
souls are wont to wander, die. This
is the fear. The greenish water tinged
with tears of sorry children, who did not
listen, but waded in, soiled skirts
held high. In spring, the rains, unleashed,

mob in and gush along its banks
with raucous cheer. In muddy rapids
faeries caught on rafts of matted
autumn leaves, dislodged from ice,
rush by, on their way to Uncle Hades'
parlour underground. From March
to June, a tune of drawn-out drowning

gurgles in the slaving mother's
anxious ears. Her children, wild and deaf
as stones to sense and harsher warnings
cannot, for the love of God, be saved
from their own folly. It is a dazzling place,
a haze of simmering light on August
afternoons, and cloaked coolly in mist

October mornings. It is the universe
where I first stepped, and where I'll go
to nestle down with worms. Though dust
by then, though bodiless, how will I
find it? How will I, formless ashes, trace
the gravel road that ends behind that house,
in that godly stream? I've asked my love

to take me, to shake me out in crystals
there, like salt, and only there to leave me
to dissolve—at last to quit this life I cannot solve.

Ghosts of Themselves

Acknowledgements

A number of the poems in this book first appeared, in earlier versions, in *ottawater 12*, *The Malahat Review*, and *Arc Poetry Magazine*. My thanks to the editors of these publications.

I am deeply grateful to Jan Zwicky for her mentorship at Sage Hill in the spring of 2014, where I began writing this book. I will always treasure the camaraderie of the other writers who were there with me: Lauren Carter, Laurie D. Graham, Basma Kavanagh, Micheline Maylor, E. Alex Pierce, Joan Shillington, and Margo Wheaton. For their comments on the manuscript as it took shape, I thank Una McDonnell, Michael Adams and, as always, Jason Creaghan, my partner in this astonishing life. Thanks, also, to the extraordinary people at Brick Books who helped usher this book into being, especially my editor, Sue Sinclair, and Alayna Munce. For financial support of this project, I am grateful to the Canada Council for the Arts, the Ontario Arts Council, and the City of Ottawa.

To my sisters, mother, aunts, and my grandmother, who now rests in peace: This book is for us.

DEANNA YOUNG is the author of four books of poetry, including *House Dreams*, which was shortlisted for the Trillium Book Award for Poetry, the Ottawa Book Award, the Archibald Lampman Award, and the ReLit Award. Born in the village of Lucan in southwestern Ontario, she grew up there, in neighbouring townships, and in the nearby city of London. She now lives in Ottawa, where she teaches poetry privately.